The Search for KING SOLOMON'S MINES

AuthorHouse™
1663 Liberty Drive
Bloomington, IN 47403
www.authorhouse.com
Phone: 1 (800) 839-8640

Published by AuthorHouse 10/12/2015

ISBN: 978-1-5049-4703-9 (sc)
ISBN: 978-1-5049-4705-3 (hc)

Library of Congress Control Number: 2015914266

Print information available on the last page.

This book is printed on acid-free paper.

author**HOUSE**®

The Search for KING SOLOMON'S MINES

DR. DIANA PRINCE

TABLE OF CONTENTS

ILLUSTRATIONS

PHOTO CREDITS

PREFACE

This book explores the truth about King Solomon's Mines. It has been over 130 years since H. Rider Haggard's adventure classic. Since that time, several spectacular movie versions have periodically kept the adventure alive.

But this is not a fable. This is not a myth. This is the true story of Solomon's Mines.

It also explores the characters in the real drama, King Solomon and the Queen of Sheba – their alliance and their love story.

Astounding sources from the ancient world verify the location of the mines, and the capital city which the Bible refers to as "Ophir, the City of Gold".

Here, also, you will see photographs of the places as they exist today.

The real story is more compelling than any novel.

Dr. Diana Prince

Chapter 1

KING SOLOMON

King Solomon was born in 967 B.C. Solomon was the Son of the Warrior King David, and the builder of the First Temple of Jerusalem.

King David had committed adultery with Bathsheba, and her husband Uriah the Hittite was murdered. Solomon was the son of David and Bathsheba.

The name "Solomon" is derived from the Hebrew word for "peace" - "Shalom".

In the book of Samuel 12:24-25, we are told that Solomon's secondary name was "Jedidiah", which means "he who is beloved by Yahweh".

He was revered as Patriarch of the Jews, and respected as a wise man by both the Gentiles and the Muslims. In the Muslim faith, he is revered as "Sulieman".

We are told in *1 Kings* 1-1 and *2 Chronicles* 1-9 that when Solomon was to ascend the throne, God appeared to him and said, "Ask what I shall give you." Solomon acknowledged himself as God's poor servant who was now to take his father's place as king. He felt the great weight of responsibility. He knew that his father had been steadfast all his life in leading his people. Solomon was paralyzed by his inexperience, and wanted to be a great man and king as his father before him. He responded to God's question that he most wanted "an understanding mind to govern thy people, that I may discern between good and evil."

God, we are told in that Biblical allegory, was so impressed that Solomon had not asked for wealth or long life or retribution against his enemies, that he promised to give Solomon all good things as well. Thus he became mighty in wealth and recognized as the wisest ruler of the ancient world. His reputation spread among all nations.

We are told,

> "And God gave Solomon wisdom and understanding beyond measure, and largeness of mind like the sand on the seashore, so that Solomon's wisdom surpassed the wisdom of all the people of the east, and all the wisdom of Egypt. For he was wiser than all other men.

(1 Kings 4: 29-31)

There is some indication that for a short time after his youth, Solomon fell away from his closeness with God, but that his relationship with God was to later be restored.

Chapter 4 of the *Book of Kings* tells us that Solomon authored 1,005 poems, which are referred to as "Songs", the most moving of which were incorporated into the *Song of Songs* or what is referred to as *Canticles*. These songs are read on the Sabbath during Passover.

The format is a lover speaking to the woman he loves. One often quoted verse is said to be a veiled reference to the Queen of Sheba, who was believed by tradition to have been his lover, and the mother of his son. In *Song of Songs*, 1:5, it appears to be the queen of Sheba speaking:

> Dark am I, yet lovely,
> daughter of Jerusalem,
> dark like the tents of Kedar,
> like the tent curtains of Solomon.

Although a thinly veiled mention of the woman having "worked in the fields" thus explaining her dark complexion, it is generally believed that the Queen of Sheba, as reported in other places, and in particular Ethiopian sources, was the black woman in this poem, and the significant figure in the life of King Solomon who bore him a son.

The response of the King in this poem shows his clear affection:

> I liken you, my darling, to a mare
> among Pharaoh's chariot horses.
> Your cheeks are beautiful with earrings,
> your neck with strings of jewels.
> *(Song of Songs, 1:9-10)*

> How beautiful you are, my darling!
> Oh, how beautiful!
> Your eyes are doves.
> *(Song of Songs, 1:15)*

The poem continues in 8 chapters. Perhaps the most beautiful passage is the lover speaking of the spring of new love:

> Arise, my darling,
> My beautiful one, come with me.
> See! The winter is past;
> The rains are over and gone.
> Flowers appear on the earth.
>
> *(Song of Songs 2:10-12)*

It is clear that it is Solomon who is the primary figure in the *Canticles*, for instance when he writes:

> Look! It is Solomon's carriage,
> escorted by sixty warriors,
> the noblest of Israel.
>
> *(Song of Songs 3:7)*

An interesting allusion occurs in the sixth song, in verses 6-9, when Solomon speaks about his multiple wives, and yet emphasizes the special character and love he has for the woman about whom he is writing:

> Sixty queens there may be
> and eighty concubines,
> and virgins beyond number;
> but my dove, my perfect one, is unique.

Could he, in fact, be speaking about the Queen of Sheba, who entered his life as a youth, loved him, and bore him a son? The son was to return years later, according to Ethiopian sources, to meet the father he had not known since birth. And Solomon is said to have celebrated that return and embraced his long absent son.

By many sources we are told that Solomon did have several wives. The primary wives lived within his court. There were about ten main wives. The main wife was the mother of the next heir of the throne. But there was a larger harem of lesser wives. In addition, there were foreign wives, possibly associated with contractual ties, and also many concubines. Most estimates suggest that these would have easily added up to more than a thousand of the King's women, who were pledged in service to him.

The uniqueness of this King, as a philosophical thinker, is apparent in an account in the *Kebra Nagast*, where Solomon is walking the streets of Jerusalem with the Queen of Sheba. They see a poor man wearing torn garments, who is sweating in the sun from his labors. Solomon tells the Queen of Sheba:

Look at this man. In what way am I superior to this man? In what am I better than this man? . . . For I, like him, am a man and dust and ashes, who tomorrow will become worms and corruption. Yet, at this moment, I appear like one who will never die.

As is his death, so is my death. As is his life, so is my life.

Then what is the use of us, the children of men, if we do not exercise kindness and love while we are on this earth?

Figure A.

**Excavation at the Mahram Bilqis, which was the Temple
of the Queen of Sheba in Marib, Yemen.**

Chapter 2

THE QUEEN OF SHEBA

Several ancient texts include accounts of the woman who has come to be known as the Queen of Sheba.

Ethiopian sources gave her the title of "Nigiste Saba". In the Hebrew *Bible*, she is Malkat Sh'va. As a South Arabian Queen in what is now Yemen, she is known by her Arabic name, Malikat Saba.

Arab legends also associate the region of Great Zimbabwe with "the city of gold" and the Queen of Sheba.

Her life is chronicled in the *Bible* in the *Book of Kings, Book II of Chronicles, Psalms,* and the *Song of Songs,* also known as the *Canticles.* She is mentioned as well in the *Septuagint.* She is also mentioned in Syrian and Ethiopian texts.

The Persians also have a counterpart of the famous Queen, but in some versions, she is portrayed as the daughter of a Chinese king. Although she is said to have had a home in Ethiopia, as well as in Arabia, she is also believed to have had a palace in southeastern Africa in what is now known as Zimbabwe. Here she had gold mines, and made her capital city in this place where the remains of the Great Zimbabwe now stand. When she visited King Solomon, the texts speak of her as being from a far distant part of the world, for Africa was infrequently traveled, even then. In our own recent times, exploration in Africa was rare up until two hundred years ago.

According to R.N. Hall in *The Ancient Ruins of Rhodesia,* he supported Thomas Baines' research that both Josephus, the historian, and Mohammed, the author of the Koran, believed that the ancient kingdom of Monomotapa (now Great Zimbabwe) was the ancient kingdom of the queen who visited Solomon.

The Queen of Sheba in Ethiopian Sources

The Queen of Sheba, by most accounts, is believed to have been born in Aksum, in what is now Ethiopia. Most dates suggest that this was around 1000 BC. However, some accounts indicate that she predated that time by over 4000 years. One of the earliest accounts from Ethiopian sources tells us about a fearsome serpent named Wainaba who terrorized the country, and prevented the people from having water unless they offered sacrifices to him.

Only one man was willing to challenge the serpent. His name was Angabo, and he cleverly devised a plan to get rid of the serpent. He prepared a goat as a sacrifice for the serpent, and had poisoned the goat beforehand. When the serpent fell dead, Angabo was given the title of King of Ethiopia. His daughter was Makeda, who is known as the Queen of Sheba, and she ruled over Ethiopia upon his death.

The mother is said to have been Queen Ismenie, who, herself, never ruled the throne. Her daughter, Makeda, became the Queen of Sheba at the age of fifteen when her father died. She was brilliant, as well as beautiful. The historian Josephus tells us that she was an ardent student of philosophy and above all things prized wisdom, which explains her fascination with King Solomon.

She was a capable diplomat and statesperson. She led her people to great prosperity, by her intervention in establishing worldwide trade, which she directed from her several palaces. Her visit to King Solomon also extended trading agreements with Israel and the Middle East.

She never married, despite some claims that she married King Solomon. She did however, bear him a son, who was her only child. She ruled her kingdom for forty years.

Biblical Sources and the Queen of Sheba

Origen identified the Queen of Sheba as the bride in the *Canticle of Canticles*, with the Queen's now famous quote, "I am very dark, but comely." (*Canticle* 1:15)

Josephus, the first century historian, said that the Queen of Sheba was a queen of both Egypt and Ethiopia.

Genesis 10:7 tells us the genealogy of the man who began the royal line of the Land of Sheba. In that account, Sheba was the son of Raamah, who was the son of Gish, who was the son of Ham, who was the son of Noah. In other words, Sheba's great-great-grandfather was the builder of the Ark during the Great Flood.

The Queen of Sheba is also mentioned in Christian sources translated from the Greek. There is a reference in *Luke* 11:31, which refers to "the Queen of the South who came from the uttermost parts of the earth." The "South" referred to the continent of Africa.

The *Kabra Nagast*, the holy book of Ethiopia, mentions Jesus speaking of this remarkable woman. It should be noted that Jesus, like Solomon, was a descendant of the House of David. In that book, Jesus is quoted as saying:

> The Queen of the South shall rise up on the Day of Judgement and shall
> dispute with, and condemn this generation who would not hear my words.
> For she came from the ends of the earth to hear the wisdom of Solomon.

The *Kabra Negast* then goes on to speak about the great perils and the difficulties taken over the three-year journey of the Queen to see Solomon. She is described as beautiful, intelligent and possessing great courage and character.

The Koran and the Queen of Sheba

She is also mentioned in the *Koran*. It describes her reaction when she first received Solomon's invitation to see him. She had heard of his great wisdom, but she also, as a reigning monarch had seen abuse of power. She knew that often, when a man came to power, it was at the expense of his subjects. In the *Koran*, she says:

> Kings, when they enter a country, despoil it, and make the noblest of its
> people its meanest, thus do they behave.

This showed she had a wisdom of her own. She was as concerned about Solomon's character and goodness, as she was about his wisdom.

The *Koran* varies in some details from the Biblical story. Islamic tradition calls the Queen of Sheba by the first name of "Bilqis", and her story is told in the *Koran*. Sura 27, verses 22-26, tell the story of how Suliman (Solomon) summoned the Queen of Sheba to his kingdom.

Solomon was gathered together with the jinn, and was talking with his menservants. At that moment, Solomon is said to have noticed the disappearance of a sacred bird, the Hoopoe, from his palace. It was believed that Solomon had an ability to communicate with such creatures. When the bird reappeared, he told Solomon that he had gone to a far-off land where he had seen a beautiful Queen sitting on a throne made of silver and gold.

The bird told him,

> I found her and her people adoring the sun instead of Allah, and the
> Shaitan has made their deeds fair-seeming to them, and thus turned them
> from the way, so they do not go aright; That they do not make obeisance
> to Allah."

Solomon then sent the Queen of Sheba an invitation for her to visit his kingdom. At first, she hesitated, and then she responded back by sending her Ambassador with a gift. Solomon scorned the gift and wrote back, "Abundance is wealth only – what Allah has given me is better than wealth," referring to his belief in God, and rejecting her worship of the sun.

The Queen of Sheba then responded to Solomon by accepting his invitation, and told him that although the trip usually took seven years, she would be there in three years. In three years, she arrived with her retinue and the gifts that she had packed onto hundreds of camels in her caravan. They were filled with gold, spices and precious stones. It is said no such marvels had been brought to the King before or since.

An interesting side story, which recurs in several other sources, is that when she arrived at Solomon's palace, the floor of the palace shone so much like glass, that she thought it was covered with water, and she lifted her skirts above her feet to avoid them touching the water.

The Queen of Sheba and Great Zimbabwe

The Queen of Sheba's many holdings included African gold mines, the greatest of which were near her capital city at what is now called Great Zimbabwe in southeastern Africa. The name refers to the large stone edifices which still emerge from the Zimbabwe landscape near a town called Masvingo.

The unique architecture has been a marvel for centuries. Massive stone walls rise without the benefit of mortar or other binding materials. They are the largest man-made structures in all of Africa south of the Sahara.

The linear rock walls curve in an elegant grace not found in other structures of its time, nor even in contemporary architecture. It was unique to this region, and totally unlike the angularity existing in most other buildings of that era. It marked a clear departure from the ordinary. Could it have been the impact of the extraordinary Queen who built it?

It was here at Great Zimbabwe that the Queen of Sheba built the largest of her palace homes. The "Great Enclosure" in this large complex is called the "Place of the Great Woman."

In this vicinity were several mines. Many of these were in the nearby Chimanimani Mountains. They continued to be a source of wealth for her people for many centuries.

Although we are not told that Solomon ever visited in this region, it was this region which was most certainly the source of the gold with which he filled his kingdom. The queen's visit had opened up new trading with Solomon's kingdom. These mines, owned by the Queen of Sheba, were located in what is now the independent nation of Zimbabwe, bordered in the north by the Zambezi River, and in the south by the Limpopo River. Trading routes were established to the east, crossing what is now Mozambique, to reach the large merchant ships at the Indian Ocean heading north to Israel and other nations.

The Relationship Between Solomon and the Queen of Sheba

The Queen of Sheba was a powerful ruler in her own right, and was known for her wealth and great beauty. She was articulate and capable. What most drew her to Solomon was his renowned gift for wisdom, which she wanted to see for herself. It is said that she brought "riddles" or situation "scenarios" to test him, and see what answers he would provide for given situations.

The *Kabra Nagast* (trans. by E. A Wallis Budge, 1932 edition) relates the Queen's first meeting with Solomon at his palace, when she tells him, "I see thy wisdom is immeasurable and thy understanding is inexhaustible."

The account in the *First Book of Kings* 10:4-7, expands on her reaction:

> When the Queen of Sheba saw all the wisdom of Solomon and the palace he had built, the food on his table, the seating of his officials, the attending servants in their roles, his Cupbearers, and the burnt offerings he made at the temple of the Lord, she was overwhelmed.

Figure B.

A portion of the Hill Complex with imposing granite rock, rises above the Great Zimbabwe hills. The greater region is bound in the north by the Zambezi River, and in the south by the Limpopo River.

She said to the king, "The report I heard in my own country about your achievements and your wisdom is true. But I did not believe these things until I came and saw with my own eyes. Indeed, not even half was told me; in wisdom and in wealth you have far exceeded the report I heard.

It is clear that this woman made an impression on Solomon as well. She was able to be direct with him and very articulate. She clearly and honestly expressed her admiration without the fawning and subservience such a man was used to hearing. She had enormous respect for his wisdom, and had enough wealth of her own to remain unintimidated by his wealth. Such a forceful expression of her honesty had to be refreshing for a man who was used to people simply doing his bidding.

We are told that he gave her whatever she wanted, in addition to the welcoming gifts he had presented her. We are told that she asked to keep some small innocuous objects, not costly items, but small mementos of her visit that she found interesting or pretty. Again, this must have been a breath of fresh air to a man who was ever surrounded by many who coveted his wealth, and whatever favor they could win from him.

Solomon's favorable impression of her is reflected in Kings 10:13:

> King Solomon gave to the Queen of Sheba all that she desired, whatever she asked besides that which was given to her by the bounty of King Solomon.

Even the evangelist Luke made mention of the Queen of Sheba in his gospel when he reprimanded the slackness of the people who would not put in the effort to listen to the words of Jesus and learn from him. Luke wrote that the Queen of Sheba had dared a great journey and hardships to hear the wisdom of Solomon, and "behold Someone greater than Solomon is here, and yet you do not listen." *Luke* 11:31.

Generations have found one of the most intriguing parts of the story about King Solomon and the Queen of Sheba to be about their personal relationship. In the *Bible*, this is not reported. There, the impressed Queen simply leaves Jerusalem and returns to her own country after verifying that Solomon is a wise man.

Several other sources speak about the King and Queen becoming lovers.

One of the most detailed versions of the story is the one in the Ethiopian *Kebra Negast*.

In that account, Solomon tells the Queen of Sheba, "I swear unto thee that I will not take thee by force." He then asks her to swear that she will not by force remove anything from his house.

She tells him that she cannot understand how a wise man can speak so foolishly, and insists that she would never steal from him, and that she had not come on her long journey to obtain riches. She told him,

"My own kingdom is as wealthy as thine, and there is nothing I wish for that I do not have. I only came here in quest of your wisdom."

But at Solomon's insistence, they made a pact that neither would take anything from the other "by force" – he would not force her to surrender her body, and she would not take any of his possessions by force.

In this version of the story, they slept separately in the same royal bed chamber. During the night, she became very thirsty and woke and saw a bowl of water the servants had left in the room. Seeing the water, she arose from the bed to get a drink.

Pretending to be asleep, King Solomon watched her. He then jumped up, grabbed her hand as she drank from the bowl, and accused her of breaking her oath to him. She asked him, "Am I accused of breaking the oath by drinking the water?" The queen relented, however, because she had taken the water. Now Solomon was also freed of his oath, and the two became lovers that night.

One of the most moving passages of the *Kebra Nagast* (E.A. Wallis Budge translation, 1932) describes Solomon's remembrance of that night:

> Solomon marveled concerning the Queen, for she was vigorous in strength, and beautiful of form, and she was undefiled in her virginity; and she had reigned for six years in her own country, and notwithstanding her gracious attraction and her splendid form, had preserved her body pure.

The story became bittersweet, since finally the lovers had to part. They each had duties to their own people, and each felt bound by those sacred duties. We are told that while the Queen of Sheba sojourned in Jerusalem, she converted from sun worship to worship the God of Solomon.

When she left, Solomon gave her, we are told, 6,000 camels and wagons, a boat, and a "vessel by which one could travel by air."

We are also told that he removed a ring from his finger and told her, "Take this that thou wilt not forget me."

She then returned home. Some accounts said that she returned home and discovered that she was pregnant with a child by Solomon. Other versions relate that after staying with Solomon at his palace for about two years, she left his palace carrying with her their infant son.

The Palaces and Holdings of the Queen of Sheba

When the Queen of Sheba visited Solomon, she is said to have had in her trade caravan 787 camels. She owned seventy-three merchant ships.

She also owned many properties. She owned more than one palace. The palace mentioned earlier at the Great Zimbabwe site is the largest, and was the capital of her many estates. The primary gold mining came from the mines near this site, and these are what are considered the "Mines of Solomon"--not for his ownership of the mines, but because these were the mines from which he imported his massive shipments of gold.

The Queen of Sheba ruled from Great Zimbabwe. The source of her great wealth was the gold that came from the mines in this region between the Zambezi and the Limpopo Rivers.

From here the gold was sent to the coast. Signs of that trade route still exist at Kilwa, the trading city on the Swahili coast, which became rich itself by association. A great mosque rose there later, made of abundant coastal coral and limestone powder from the coral. In the 1500's the Portuguese spoke of it as a magnificent city, and its wealth had long been associated with the gold trade coming from Great Zimbabwe, located 1500 kilometers inland.

Midway between Great Zimbabwe and Kilwa on the coast was the city of Rhapta. It too became wealthy from the gold. However, the specialty at Rhapta came from the skilled goldsmiths and artisans who molded and shaped gold treasures. These were later packed aboard ships at Kilwa and were exported to regions as far away as India and China.

The Queen of Sheba was an exceptional diplomat. From the age of fifteen, she astutely ruled her kingdom. She met King Solomon when she was in her early twenties. She had the knowledge and skill to create a network of trade that ensured her country's economic stability.

One of her palaces was at Khor Ruri in Salalah, in what is now Oman. It is located in the region of Dhofar which is famous for supplying most of the world's frankincense. Frankincense was one of the gifts purported to have been given to King Solomon by the Queen of Sheba.

The Queen of Sheba had another palace at Aksum in Ethiopia. The remains of this large palace can be seen today. Although parts of the upper wall are missing, it is possible to count over 40 rooms outlined in the layout of the remaining stone walls. The site was excavated over a nine-year period from 1999 to 2008 by archaeologists from the University of Hamburg in Germany. They determined that the palace is built with an alignment to the star Sirius. The remaining rock walls show a similarity to the small fitted rock used at Great Zimbabwe, but they are constructed in the typical angular architecture, rather than the free flowing elliptical walls that grace the structures at Great Zimbabwe.

Aksum is Ethiopia's oldest city, and it was claimed to have been the birthplace of the Queen of Sheba. It was, according to tradition, founded by the great-grandson of Noah, Aksumawi. Today Aksum is considered the holiest of cities according to the Ethiopian Orthodox Church.

The Queen of Sheba is also said to have lived for part of the year at Marib, which was the capital of the land of Sheba. This was the land also known as "Saba", and more commonly referred to as the land of the Sabaeans, in the region which today is called Yemen. It was at one time known as Abyssinia. There are also sources in Arabian history which allude to powerful queens who ruled in Arabia in ancient times.

Between 1200 and 1000 BC, a temple had been built at Marib in honor of the Queen of Sheba. She was sometimes associated with the ancient goddess Astarte, who is often depicted with a lioness. Called the Awam Temple, it was the largest in South Arabia. It is under excavation. Its striking architecture consisted of a great oval pavilion flanked by a circle of massive pillars. Even in its partially excavated state today, it is still a stunning temple.

Another temple was built in her honor in Marib around 1000 BC. It is called the Mahram Bilqis, or the Temple of the Queen of Sheba. This is said to have been built to house her treasures. It was built on thirty-seven acres, and was first excavated in the 1950's. At this point, the sub-structure and flooring have been exposed down to the layer built in 700 BC.

Her palace at Saba is also in the process of being excavated. Unfortunately, current discord in the Middle East has brought the work to a halt.

Another great architectural marvel was built at Merib. A great dam was constructed in the 1000 BC era, and some attribute it to the Queen of Sheba. It was able, by a complex irrigation network and ingenious planning, to turn the desert into an arable land of fruit trees and crops.

This dam was 50 feet in height, and 2100 feet in length. That length was double the length of the Hoover Dam. This dam was in use for over fourteen centuries.

Unfortunately, on May 31, 2015, part of the dam was severely damaged by Saudi Forces who were engaged in airstrikes against Shiite forces in Yemen.

Figure C.

These walls of the Great Enclosure are part of the palace of the Queen of Sheba near Masvingo, Zimbabwe.

Chapter 3

THE CITY OF GOLD

When the Queen of Sheba visited King Solomon, she is said to have brought him 120 talents of gold. He is elsewhere said to have imported 666 talents of gold per year from abroad. The *Bible* and tradition mention the city of Ophir. Both the *Bible* and the ancient world spoke about it as "The City of Gold." Ophir was believed to be the source of wealth, and specifically gold, which the Queen of Sheba brought to the Israelite king.

Other traditions addressing the city of Ophir stated that it was at "the nethermost regions of the world." This should be a major clue in deciphering the location.

One of the places suggested as the city of Ophir was the South Arabian Kingdom of Saba, located near the Marib oasis in what is today known as Yemen. That is where the Queen of Sheba resided part of the time. The Sabeans who lived in Saba were known to have visited the seacoast town of Sofala in south eastern Africa, from which they brought back large shipments of gold. These merchants, with their sophisticated trading routes excelled in bringing that gold to market, but the gold did not originate with them, nor was it mined by them.

It was rather Great Zimbabwe that was the City of Gold known as Ophir.

There are indications in the *Bible* that King David had acquired significant gold from Ophir, from mining operations which were already well established in his lifetime. The gold mines in Great Zimbabwe were in operation long before the time of King David, and were still in operation in the time of Solomon and the Queen of Sheba.

R. N. Hall and W. G. Neal prepared a report on Great Zimbabwe and other sites in *The Ancient Ruins of Rhodesia: Monomotapa Imperium*, published by Methuen and Company (London, 1903). In the report, Hall confirmed that Rhodesia was "the land from which the gold of Ophir was obtained" and "the source of King Solomon's gold."

Hall also stated that the period during which Great Zimbabwe was erected "coincided with the same period that Biblical references were made about the gold of Ophir." He stated that in that period of time, "millions of pounds of gold" had been extracted at Great Zimbabwe, and that, "No part of the then known world yielded such overwhelming evidence of extensive, continuous, and successful ancient gold mining operations."

Many archaeologists suggest that the Great Zimbabwe structures were constructed in two primary building periods. Estimates of the older period vary from 8,000 to 5,000 BC. The more current period is generally held to have been between 2,000 BC to 800BC, which would put them in the same chronological time frame as Solomon and the Queen of Sheba.

These dates differ greatly from the estimates of some recent European archaeologists who have visited the site in the past hundred years. Some of them estimate the structures to have been built as recently as the twelfth century. These estimates contradict the much earlier evidence of active mines at Great Zimbabwe based on many ancient sources primarily from Egypt, Ethiopia, Yeman and the Biblical texts.

Southeast Africa, and in particular the vicinity of Great Zimbabwe, have a significant number of mines which show evidence of having had a massive amount of gold removed over thousands of years. South Africa, overall, is still the largest gold producer in the world, and it is estimated that even in recent times almost 80 percent of world gold supplies have come from Africa.

Mr. Telford Edwards, considered an expert on the mines of Rhodesia (now Zimbabwe), estimated that:

> The value of the ancient output of gold at Zimbabwe was not less than $375,000,000. There is little room for doubt that the Ophir of the Bible, from which Solomon drew such vast quantities of gold is Zimbabwe, and the ruins at Great Zimbabwe mark the center of the mining operations.
>
> (From "Africa-Past and Present" by Rev. J.G. Vaughan, in *The Missionary Review of the World*, Vol. 32, 1909, Funk & Wagnalls, N.Y.)

Yemen, Arabia and the cities of the Assyrians are clearly eliminated from being the fabled "Ophir", which was the city of gold. None of them had notable gold deposits, and none of them would have met the specification of requiring "three years of travel to reach Jerusalem", which was the specified time frame required to transport the gold from Ophir to King Solomon. Also, the Arabian countries would not have been described as being "from the nether parts of the world." That would, however, have applied to the distant mines of southeastern Africa.

The Queen of Sheba managed to reach King Solomon in three years, according to Ethiopian accounts. It is also mentioned in the *Bible* that "every three years" Solomon received his vast shipments of gold. Ancient sources wrote:

The King had a fleet of trading ships at sea along with the ships of Hiram. Once
every three years it returned carrying gold, silver and ivory.

First Book of Kings, 10:22

The Queen of Sheba was associated at that time with vast holdings in Egypt, Ethiopia, Marib in what is now Yemen, but most importantly with the mines at Great Zimbabwe. She is said to have established her capital at Great Zimbabwe.

Ezekial 27 also mentions that the traders of Sheba were very rich in gold, spices and precious stones, and gives further evidence of The Queen of Sheba's involvement and ownership of the mines at Great Zimbabwe.

The Queen of Sheba also had a great fleet of ships. They landed at the coastal port of Sofala, where the merchants would load the gold brought from the inland region around Great Zimbabwe. They would then set out on the lengthy and exhaustive voyages to their homes in the north, where the gold was loaded onto camel caravans. Then the gold shipments were delivered to their final destinations. The process was rugged, sometimes dangerous, and not for the faint-hearted.

Of these cities mentioned as a source of gold, none except for Great Zimbabwe could be considered at the "nethermost ends of the earth" even in Solomon's time. A cursory look at the map will note that even the Arabian cities were accessible in a relatively short period of time. The Arabs were prolific traders and had a sturdy merchant fleet. But among their own Arab cities, no city existed that would have yielded the gold described in the ancient texts.

The "nethermost ends of the earth" would point to the least explored areas of southeastern Africa, and specifically the rich gold mines of Great Zimbabwe.

There is evidence that the Queen of Sheba had palaces at both Ethiopia as well as at Great Zimbabwe, although the residence at Ethiopia was in no way as extensive and elaborate as the one at the Zimbabwe stone complex. Also, the gold mines near Zimbabwe would have been the primary source of her gold exports.

No other location so fits the description of Ophir as the site at the Great Zimbabwe Ruins which are located today near the town of Masvingo, formerly called Fort Victoria by the British.

The ancestors of the modern Shona tribe were the Bantu, who have occupied the site for centuries. They are credited with being the builders of the architectural marvel called Great Zimbabwe. Today, in southeast Zimbabwe, the massive stone walls curve across a green landscape of almost 2,000 acres – 1,800 to be exact. The Shona tribe still traces its roots to those early times which have been treasured and preserved in their verbal and written folklore, legends and traditions.

This complex of stone walls and towers, constructed without the use of mortar, spreads in a unique linear style, across the rich green landscape, like a slim ribbon of rock. And yet, the gracefulness belies the incredible strength of the walls, some reaching up to 14 feet in thickness. This is the largest man-made stone complex south of the Sahara Desert.

Further evidence of valuable gold resources in this area was what has come to be called the "Golden Kingdom of Mapungubwe". It was thriving in about the twelfth century AD. Its location was said to be where the "hill emerges" south of Great Zimbabwe, and across the border in what is now the country of South Africa. Here goldsmiths and gold workers processed the abundant gold available in the surrounding region.

Additional evidence of the extensive gold trade in the area, was the city of Manyikeni, a midpoint halfway between Sofala at the coast and Great Zimbabwe. The name "Manyikeni" means literally "a place people give to each other", referring to an exchange or bargaining network. The main occupation here was that of the "gold broker". These people made trades, contracts and arrangements for the gold distribution. They worked closely with the merchants involved in the gold industry.

One of the most sophisticated mining operations, and one of the richest, was located near Lake Mutirikwe in the vicinity of Great Zimbabwe.

Tome Lopes, who had accompanied Vasco de Gama in his extensive travels in 1502, journeyed into inner Africa. He was the first European to identify the vast gold trade at Great Zimbabwe, and to make a supposition that this might have a connection to the Biblical city of Ophir.

In 1552, a Portuguese, Joao de Baros heard about the city, which was said to have been ruled at one time by the Queen of Sheba. He heard stories from Arab traders, who had carried on trade in the inland regions of Zimbabwe. In this region bound in the north by the Zambezi River, and in the south by the Limpopo River, there was a rich agricultural community. But there were also extensive mining deposits of gold reaching intermittently from what is now Johannesburg to the site of the massive House of Stone now known as Great Zimbabwe, and its elaborate compound near modern day Masvingo.

In his book called *Decades of Asia*, Baros chronicled the stories of Portuguese exploits in India and in southeast Africa as relayed to him by soldiers and merchants.

Although Baros had not visited the site himself, he kept in touch with other Portuguese merchants and wayfarers who had seen the stone city, and were also convinced that Great Zimbabwe was, in fact, the ancient city of Ophir.

It was almost twenty years later in 1572 that Francisco Barreto was sent by the Portuguese Dom Sebastian to venture into Monomotapa, which was the name of the empire established at Great Zimbabwe. His orders were to take over the legendary gold mines. Before this happened, however, he and almost all of his men died of the malaria prevalent in the region.

To complete the mission which Barreto had been unable to do, his successor Vasco Fernandez Homen traveled inland via Sofala, and found the mines in Manica, not far from the imposing structures of Great Zimbabwe. He was to discover, however, that some of the mines he explored had been mined for centuries, and most of their wealth had been expended.

This suggested two things. One was that the time period of the mining at Manica had indeed covered many centuries of production, a much longer period of time than the archaeologists had estimated, and that is why the mines were now so depleted. If these deposits had been mined since Solomon's time, this would make sense. The second conclusion was that depletion of that precious commodity was more than likely to have been the real reason that the gold trading activity had seen its demise in the 1400's, and ushered in the end of the long-running era of gold at Great Zimbabwe.

R. Gayre in his book *Origin of the Zimbabwean Civilization*, printed by Galaxy Press in Rhodesia, in 1972, estimated that more than 20 million ounces of gold had been extracted from the ground in the mines near Great Zimbabwe.

It was not until 1867 that Europeans would again travel inland to see this fabled city for themselves. Alexander Merensky was one of the first. At that time it was called Monomotapa, named after an illustrious chief, Mwene Mototo who had united the many Zimbabwe tribes into solidarity three hundred years earlier. Mototo, whose name was the basis for the empire of Monomotapa at Great Zimbabwe, knew that an alliance of the many tribes was vital if they were to flourish in the future.

Based on Merensky's account, Karl Gottlieb Mauch explored this area in 1871. In addition to the name "Monomotapa", it was also variously referred to at that time as "Symbaoe" and "Zimbaoche". He was fascinated with the great stone structures which he found there. From the local Karanga tribe he heard that the main enclosure was called "Imbahuru", which translates to "The House of the Great Woman." He was convinced that the great woman spoken about was the Queen of Sheba, and that this was one of her palaces. He was also of the opinion that the nearby gold mines, although now much depleted, had been the source of the gold she had brought to King Solomon.

In 1892, Theodore Bent under the auspices of the Royal Geographical Society did excavations at Great Zimbabwe. In his book *The Ruined Cities of Mashonaland*, he mentioned that the massive elliptical circle at Great Zimbabwe resembled a similar construction in one of the temples built by the Queen of Sheba at Marib in Arabia. The circle at Great Zimbabwe is called the Great Enclosure. It was also connected with legends of the "Great Woman" and the archaeologist Bent believed they referred to the Queen of Sheba who is said to have built it.

Alexander Wilmot in his study *Monomotapa, Rhodesia: It's Monuments and Its History*, republished by the British Library in 2011, quoted Theodore Bent's observations at Great Zimbabwe as of particular interest. In one description, Bent recorded in his excavations of Great Zimbabwe:

> To the south of the Temple, a flight of steps led down to the gold-smelting furnaces and the caves.

This reinforces Wilmot's idea that this was evidence of the extensive gold production that had, in ancient times, made its way to Solomon and the great kingdoms to the north.

Wilmot, like German archaeologist Mauch firmly believed that Great Zimbabwe was the ancient city of gold – the fabled Ophir.

Wilmot also found that Mauch's field observations gave additional evidence:

> The ruins at Great Zimbabwe and other smaller zimbabwes are always found near gold workings; they are built in the same way, using granite hewn into small blocks . . .and are put together without mortar.

Wilmot also believed that the building of Great Zimbabwe pre-dated Solomon's reign in Jerusalem, and he was very unsatisfied with the estimates that tried to fit the building, growth and demise of the Great Zimbabwe into a five hundred year period that ended as recently as the fourteenth century A. D.

He insisted, "We can scarcely be wrong in concluding that the oldest of the Zimbabwes were erected before the ninth century B.C." This would confirm that the mines were in full operation during the time of Solomon and the Queen of Sheba.

He observed, on one occasion, that some of the first diggings of the British South African Company during the reign of Queen Victoria were probably the same mines of Ophir mined a thousand years before Christ.

Wilmot stated in *Monomotapa*,

> The preponderance of evidence is decidedly in favor of the Ophir mentioned in Scripture having been this inland empire (Great Zimbabwe), inland from the Sofala coast, in the country of Monomotapa.

Wilmot was not alone in his belief that Great Zimbabwe was the ancient city of scripture. He pointed to several contemporaries who shared his views, including Bruce, A'Ancielle, Quatremere and Guillain.

Independence for Zimbabwe

On the long road toward independence, a number of things happened in Zimbabwe. Exploitative and punitive policies were enacted against the native population of Zimbabwe. The people were even robbed of their country's name, which was renamed South Rhodesia after Cecil Rhodes. Under Cecil Rhodes' policies and during 30 years of rule by the British South Africa Company, some serious setbacks occurred for the native population. In 1923, Southern Rhodesia became a self-governing colony, it was not until 1980 that it was granted independence from English rule.

Peter Garlake was to make an immeasurable difference in setting the cultural record straight in Zimbabwe. Garlake, born in Capetown, South Africa in 1934 had been educated by Jesuits at St. George's College and later attended Cape Town University. He did some excavation work at Manekweni in Mozambique. After marrying Margaret Mallet, they went to Harare, then called Salisbury, where he was employed by the British Institute in East Africa.

He was given the position of "Inspector of Monuments" in Zimbabwe. He later wrote a book called *Great Zimbabwe* (Thames & Am; Hudson, 1973) in which he spoke of the Great Zimbabwe Complex and its "imposing grandeur". This book was later republished by the Zimbabwe Publishing House in 1982.

In 1965, government instructions overseeing the Zimbabwe sites changed. The new directives demanded that any sites claimed to have been built by Africans required equal acknowledgment that they could also have been built by foreigners. They implied that the Phoenicians or other ancient visitors had built the structures at Great Zimbabwe. In effect, the "party line" was that these monuments could not have been built by the Africans themselves.

Peter Garlake was appalled by this deception intended to discredit the Black populace from having created their own work. This mass censorship and revisionist history which the elite Cecil Rhodes had imposed on the public denied categorically that the monumental structures had been built by the Blacks. He insisted that the monuments must have been the work of foreigners. He refused to acknowledge that the African natives had the sophistication and skills to have achieved these feats.

Despite pressure by the Rhodesian government's prime minister Ian Smith, Peter Garlake insisted that the building of such monuments as Great Zimbabwe had been done by Black ancestors of the Shona, and he proved this point categorically. Because of this, the government stripped him of his position as Inspector of Monuments, and forced him to leave the country in 1970. Forced to leave Zimbabwe, he went to Nigeria for awhile, and later to London. After Zimbabwe received its independence in 1980, he returned the following year in 1981 to lecture at the University of Zimbabwe.

Further evidence of a concerted effort to undermine the African origins of Great Zimbabwe, was revealed in Julie Frederiks' excellent "Harare Oral Traditions Project", compiled in the book *None But Ourselves*, published by Anvil Press in 1982.

In that book, Paul Sinclair, who was the archaeologist stationed at Great Zimbabwe, stated how the directors of the Museums and Monuments Organization had told him to be very careful about what he said when talking to the press about the origins of Great Zimbabwe. He was told that the government was putting pressure on them to withhold the correct information. He stated,

> Censorship of guidebooks, museum displays and school textbooks, was a daily occurrence. Once a member of the Museum Board of Trustees threatened me with losing my job if I said publicly that blacks had built Zimbabwe.

In 1973, the *Encyclopedia Rhodesia* stated that the ruins at Great Zimbabwe were in fact "King Solomon's Palace" – an attempt to show foreign influence in creating it. This author believes that Great Zimbabwe was definitely not Solomon's palace, but that it was one of the palaces of the Queen of Sheba.

There is no evidence that Solomon ever visited or owned the mines at Great Zimbabwe. The sole ownership and accomplishments therein belonged to the Africans of Zimbabwe, and, for a time, they were under the rule and auspices of the African Queen of Sheba.

However the mines at Great Zimbabwe are without question the source of King Solomon's gold. These mines were the destination of his fleet of ships who brought him his gold from the ends of the earth. These mines were also the source of the gold given to him by the Queen of Sheba.

Figure D

The towers at the entrance to the Great Enclosure at Great Zimbabwe. The rocks in the massive towers have been fitted together without mortar or other binding materials.

Chapter 4

FOLLOW THE GOLD

Solomon is reputed by some sources to have received 13 and one-half tons of gold each year – weighed and determined in "talents", which was the standard measurement. However, in the first book of *Kings* 10:14, the figure is put at 666 talents of gold acquired every year. This would be 25 tons, or 23 metric tons.

Other sources have put the estimated total of gold mined in all of history at 181,881 tons.

The gold trade has, down through the ages, played a significant part in the Great Zimbabwe area. The Queen of Sheba had a major investment in the gold trade here, and she made Great Zimbabwe her capital city. In addition, her vast holdings extended to a palace in Aksum, Ethiopia and a palace in what is now Yemen. The remains of these palaces can still be seen today.

All of southern Africa has a long history of mines dating even, in some cases, to prehistoric times. Thirty miles north of Johannesburg evidence has been found of mining activity which was estimated by scholars to have been producing gold as early as 8,000 BC.

In looking at gold mining in the vicinity of Great Zimbabwe, we can see that the mining and processing of gold were key industries in the nearby kingdom of Mapungubwe. That kingdom was estimated to have been built around 1,075 A.D., and was located south of Great Zimbabwe. It maintained a flourishing gold trade, and had regular trading routes with both Kilwa Kisiwani and Rhapta on the east coast of Africa. The population in Mapungubwe at that time was believed to have numbered over 5,000 people.

And even prior to the year 1,000, the culture designated as the K2 culture predated the coming of the Mapungubwe kings. This culture called the Kopje culture based their economy on the gold and ivory trades. This further shows a continuing and sustained gold-based economy that concurs with the records that Great Zimbabwe and these other successful mining ventures operated from an age much older than the usual dates given. Of these, the elegant complex at Great Zimbabwe was by far the oldest.

One literal Shona translation of "Mapungubwe" is "rocks of the bateleur eagle" -that same bird once featured prominently on the pillars at Great Zimbabwe, and now appears on the Zimbabwe flag.

In 1933 some bodies were exhumed from Mapungubwe Hill. One couple, appearing to be royalty, were found buried with gold bangles and beads. Again, a long distinguished history, and ties to the gold trade, would suggest this area—linked with the mines that flourished here during the time of the Queen of Sheba – were the primary source of her great wealth.

During the excavation of Great Zimbabwe, prior to 1903, R. N. Hall, in his report *The Ancient Ruins of Rhodesia*, confirmed that the presence of gold processing sites had been identified on the premises of Great Zimbabwe. He stated that:

> The ancient gold-smelting furnaces were not built up from the ground, but sunk into the floors. Sir John Willoughby found three of these holes close together in the floors of an elliptical ruin, identified as the No. 3 ruin halfway between the Elliptical temple and the Acropolis.

Also, the exotic and unique construction of Great Zimbabwe did not belong to a commoner, nor was it meant to be some temporary encampment. The fact that some legends link the edifice with a commanding and notable "Great Woman" suggests that this place was very likely the palace of the Queen of Sheba. Her palace in Ethiopia was not as elegant and distinguished as the Great Zimbabwe architecture which still stands today on this remote landscape.

It is certain that the age of Great Zimbabwe, has not been positively established. Finding remnants of tribes inhabiting the area and leaving artifacts of their own in more recent ages, only proves that the buildings and grounds were from time to time used for dwellings and rituals by more recent cultures. And finding proof of those who settled in, and temporarily used the complex, does nothing to verify the original building date. Their artifacts clearly reflect their later occupation of the grounds, but do not give us the original dates of Great Zimbabwe.

There is however, nothing that would suggest that the original builders were anything but skilled native Africans who produced archaeological wonders in southern Africa, just as the Africans in the north were the skilled architects and pyramid builders centuries earlier.

There is evidence of many gold mines having existed in a wide swathe from what is today Johannesburg eastward to Great Zimbabwe.

R. Gayre in his book *The Origin of the Zimbabwean Civilization* estimates that at least 20 million ounces of gold were extracted from the area around Great Zimbabwe.

This is confirmed by John Hays Hammond, an American engineer who went to Zimbabwe to work with Cecil Rhodes at the British South Africa Company. He had complete charge over the gold mines in both South Africa and Zimbabwe under Rhodes. He acknowledged that millions of pounds of gold had already been removed from the mines in the area, testifying to the long history of mining involvement in this region.

Certainly if such mining took place, it would not be unthinkable that this was the source of the Queen of Sheba's magnificent display of gold as a tribute to Solomon when she visited him in Biblical times. Active mining existed since the earliest of times, and reflects man's long fascination and quest for gold.

The Greek *Periplus*, written in the first century was a document of ports, landmarks and distance computations vital to ship captains during a voyage. It was essentially a nautical roadmap with comments. It noted that in 35 A.D., King Kharabit of Sheba controlled East Africa to "an indefinite extent" with respect to the mines at Great Zimbabwe. This is clear evidence of the presence of Sheba's merchants long involvement in the mining activities of Zimbabwe.

In 1502 AD, while in the port of Sofala, the Portuguese explorers heard of a wonderful rich mine located inland at Great Zimbabwe, and referred to it, even then, as King Solomon's Mines.

In 1505, the Moors spoke of ancient stories about the gold from Great Zimbabwe being taken down the Zambezi River to the trading depots of the Queen of Sheba at the coast. This gave further proof that this was the origin of her gold.

Certainly Ethiopia's gold trade was active in Solomon's time, as written records have confirmed. The historian Herodotus, in 500 BC spoke of Ethiopia involved in the gold trade. However the mines they frequented were those of Zimbabwe. The Ethiopians were the most prolific merchants and traders trafficking in gold. The mines of Zimbabwe appear to have been actively involved in the gold markets from ancient times. The operations and logistics were centered at Great Zimbabwe. Great Zimbabwe directed the gold trade at least two thousand years before the fourteenth century. It was in a position to furnish both gold and other traded goods not only to Solomon, but also to other nations.

The Zimbabwe gold producers collaborated with the Ethiopian traders. After gold was culled from the mines, it was shipped eastward on the Zambezi River to Kilwa for processing. It then sailed in the Indian Ocean from Sofala northwards aboard large merchant ships.

King David, the father of Solomon, had already been importing from the mines of Great Zimbabwe long before his son Solomon met the Queen of Sheba.

The exhaustion of the gold mines has been suggested as one of the main reasons for the abandonment of the Great Zimbabwe site after a long period of continued habitation. This is only likely if the gold trade had been going in these mines for a significant period of time. Some of the mines could have been exhausted since the time of Solomon, but certainly not in the 500-year period suggested by the alleged "rise and fall" of Great Zimbabwe asserted by some proponents.

At Great Zimbabwe, the Great Enclosure was called Imbahuru, which means the "Place of the Great Woman" in the Karala dialect of the Shona people. It is very likely that the woman they are referring to was the Queen of Sheba. No other historical figure comes close to matching her civic achievements. Not content to manage her country from the safe distance of her throne, she took an unparalleled role in establishing and maintaining trade routes. And she, herself, embarked on the three-year journey to meet with Solomon, rather than leaving that to her envoys.

It is not mere conjecture that the grand architecture at Great Zimbabwe could have been her own residence there. We know that she also maintained a palace near Aksum in Ethiopia, which can still be seen today. Although similar to Great Zimbabwe in some of its courtyards and rock walls, it is not as extensive as Great Zimbabwe, nor is it as magnificent.

The exhaustion of the gold mines in the vicinity of Great Zimbabwe have been suggested as one of the main reasons for the abandonment of that site suddenly and inexplicably around 1400 A.D. This is even more likely if the gold had been systematically mined since the time of Solomon.

The erroneous belief that the structures at Great Zimbabwe were only built in the eleventh century, and then took an additional three hundred years to complete, before being completely abandoned shortly afterwards makes little sense. And if the depletion of the existing gold in local mines near Great Zimbabwe was the reason for the exodus from that region in 1400A.D., that short time frame for active mining could not have depleted the gold reserves in that area.

The explorer, Vasco Homen, expressed great surprise in 1574 to find that the mines in Manica near Great Zimbabwe were totally depleted. He knew immediately that only a significant period of mining over several centuries could have caused that, and this convinced him that the mines dated to ancient times.

Today, of the current ten largest gold-producing mines in the world, three of them are in Africa. One is the South Deep mine at Johannesburg in South Africa, considered the second largest in the world. Another is the Mponeng mine, near Carletonville, South Africa, which is the deepest mine in the world. And the third is the Obuasi mine in Ghana in West Africa.

This shows that Africa is still a major gold producer, having nearly a third of existing significant deposits. So, too, in ancient times the gold mines of Africa were the most likely source of King Solomon's famous imports of gold. This makes the case for the mines near Great Zimbabwe being the most likely candidate for being the source of King Solomon's gold.

The remaining seven contenders on the above-mentioned list of current top gold producers are mines in Indonesia, New Guinea, Siberia, the Dominican Republic, Western Australia, a site on the border between Chile and Argentina, and a Nevada mine in the United States.

None of these countries were even in existence in Solomon's time, and clearly were not in any geographical proximity to have been the source of his gold.

Finally, an examination of the other places which have been proposed as possible locations for Solomon's mines include mines in Israel, Yemen or Arabia. It is clear that Solomon's first choice would have been the gold in Africa, where it was plentiful then as it is now.

But the mines located at Eilat in Israel, Yemen or Arabia which are considered as the possible sources of Solomon's gold do not meet the Biblical descriptions that referred to them as existing in the "nethermost regions of the world," far from Solomon's palace in Jerusalem.

The paragraphs above suggest that the "Mines of Solomon" were most likely in Africa, which still maintains a significant position in gold deposits, making a very reasonable argument that King Solomon's gold came from the mines near Great Zimbabwe.

Figure E.

At sunset, the entrance to the historic Hill Complex at Great Zimbabwe overlooks the vast terrain that served as a gold mining and processing center even before the days of the Biblical King David. Here at Great Zimbabwe was the African city of "Ophir", which the Queen of Sheba made her capital city.

Chapter 5

SON OF SOLOMON AND THE QUEEN OF SHEBA

Traditions say that when the Queen of Sheba returned from Jerusalem and her sojourn with King Solomon, that she carried with her an infant, a son by King Solomon.

Some believe this son was Menelik I. When he grew to adulthood, he set out to meet his father, and was joyously received by Solomon. As proof of his identity he carried with him the ring which Solomon had presented to his mother over two decades earlier. Menelik studied the Judaic religion and the Law of Moses for the three years that he remained with his father in Jerusalem.

There was apparently a strong resemblance between Solomon and his son. This caused some discord in Solomon's kingdom, and the people urged Solomon to send Menelik home. Solomon, however, reluctant to let his long-separated son depart, specified that each of the high priests would have to send away their own eldest son with Menelik if he were sent away. In addition, Solomon asked that from each tribe of Israel, 1,000 men must also accompany Menelik. So over 12,000 men set out for Menelik's home at Aksum, Ethiopia.

Azariah, the son of Zadok, one of the high priests, had been told in a dream that he should take the Ark of the Covenant with them. In its place he put a replica of the Ark. When Menelik found out what had been done, he was angry, but was persuaded to continue on his journey.

When Solomon discovered the theft, he sent an army in pursuit, but was told in a dream to leave the Ark of the Covenant with his son. He then relented, and told the high priests to keep the disappearance of the Ark a secret.

When Menelik reached Aksum, he established the Solomonic Dynasty, and the kingdom converted to Judaism and the Law that had been given by Moses.

In the fourth century, when some of the people converted to Christianity, the leaders resisted, and continued to practice Judaism. This practice of Judaism continued in an unbroken line up until the 1974 revolution which signaled the end of the line of Ethiopian kings. During all that time, the leaders claimed their direct descent from King Solomon. This Solomonic Dynasty of kings had spanned over 3,000 years of a direct reign, and passed the kingship through over 200 generations.

The Ark of the Covenant is revered by the Ethiopian Orthodox Church. It now rests in Aksum, Ethiopia. Since 1965, the Ark of the Covenant has been in a small chapel built by Emperor Haile Selassie in the Church of St. Mary of Zion. The Church of St. Mary at Aksum was originally a Christian Church.

A monk is appointed for life to guard the Ark, and he is the only one allowed to go into this chapel. The monk must select his successor before he dies.

A replica of the Ark of the Covenant called the "tabot" can be found in every Ethiopian Orthodox Tewahedo Church today. This signifies that the church is consecrated.

The palace of the Queen of Sheba at Aksum, and the famous baths adjoining it can still be seen today at Aksum.

Menelik was called the "Son of the Wise". Upon the death of his mother, he assumed the kingship with the title of "Emperor" as well as "King of Kings", referring to his higher rule over all of the other Ethiopian kings.

In the Ethiopian holy book, the *Kebra Nagast*, the entire story of the Queen of Sheba and King Solomon is related. One of the sources was an ancient manuscript found in Hagia Sofia Church in Turkey. It also documents the account of Solomon's son with the Queen of Sheba, Menelik, and the account of how the Ark of the Covenant was taken away to Ethiopia.

Another tradition is that the son of King Solomon and the Queen of Sheba was Nebuchadnezzar. This was first suggested by Ben Sira in the eleventh century. This would not appear to be accurate, since Nebuchadnezzar was the Babylonian king who led his forces against King Solomon and destroyed Jerusalem in 587 B.C. There are no corresponding texts or sources to suggest that ill will existed between King Solomon and his son. On the contrary, when reunited in the young man's adulthood, the King graciously and happily welcomed the young man.

Figure F. (Following Page)

**Ancestors of the Shona Tribe built the wall around "Imbahuru" which
in the Kalanga dialect means "The House of the Great Woman."
The wall is 820 feet in length, and has a height of 32 feet.**

Chapter 6

GREAT ZIMBABWE SITE

The remnants of an ancient civilization rise above the green landscape of Zimbabwe. Known today as "Great Zimbabwe", it lies in the southeastern hills of Zimbabwe near Lake Mutirikwe. During the late Iron Age it was the capital of the region.

The ancestors of the Shona called the Bantu built Great Zimbabwe. Estimates place the original building in the ninth century, but more recent evaluations based on several ancient sources, place the building many centuries earlier.

Concealed for years in the fertile land between the Zambezi River to the north, and the Limpopo River to the south, it is only in the last few centuries that the structure has attracted world attention. Now a UNESCO site, protected and preserved under the auspices of the United Nations, there is an effort for archaeologists to define its significance, and decipher its ancient past.

There are records that confirm that the earliest people in this region had a rich agricultural heritage. The Gokomere culture, developed by the ancestors of the modern Shona, are known to have farmed and mined in the area between the fourth and seventh centuries AD.

Other sources corroborate that mining has been carried out in this region since the earliest times. By the fourteenth century A.D., it is believed that over 18,000 people occupied the immediate region around the site that is now called Great Zimbabwe. Some estimates have indicated that the actual number could have been as high as 25,000 people.

The first mention of Great Zimbabwe was by Vicente Pegado in 1531. He was captain of the Portuguese garrison at Sofala, who referred to it as "Symbaoe" which meant "court". In the Zezuru dialect of the Shona it was "dzima-hwe" which means "stone house".

Although European explorers first came to this area in the early 1500's, they did not settle here. With few exceptions, another three centuries would pass before Europeans again ventured into what is now Zimbabwe, and established their own settlements.

The unfortunate truth is that the white man's early visits to this area were charged with self interest to the point of exploitation. There is no question that the colonial rule brought a rewriting of history to some extent, due to the mindset of the newcomers that this land was theirs for the taking.

One serious error was the attempt to downplay the fact that the African people, themselves, were the architects of the thriving kingdom of Great Zimbabwe. In addition to the local Africans, further African influences which contributed to the success of this area included merchants and investors from such places as Ethiopia and northern Africa who were instrumental in making Zimbabwe a major trading point for gold. It was clearly the African people, themselves, who built this prosperous kingdom.

As recently as this past century, many newcomers tried to attribute the buildings of Great Zimbabwe to the Phoenicians, to visitors from the Middle East, or to anyone other than the African people themselves. This was even done through edicts propagated under Cecil Rhodes' authority which denied that the native people had any part in the design and building of Great Zimbabwe. The disproportionate distribution of wealth to the white settlers also showed the further disenfranchisement of the African people from their own heritage.

Many believe that Great Zimbabwe is without doubt the City of Gold known in Biblical scriptures as "Ophir". Also, it is considered the center of ancient mines which provided gold to both Solomon and the Queen of Sheba. From Great Zimbabwe, the gold was transported across Mozambique to Sofala at the coast. From there it was loaded onto merchant ships and sent north from Africa to the great kingdoms of the world. There is strong evidence for all of this.

Dating the Great Zimbabwe Ruins

It is almost impossible to correctly date the Great Zimbabwe structures near Masvingo for the number of reasons mentioned earlier. Chapter 6, however, gives ample evidence of ancient mining operations carried out in this area two thousand years before Christ. Other sources cite significantly greater timelines of gold production in this area reaching back to the dawn of civilization itself.

The current estimates, largely published in the past century, are based on inconsistent and incomplete information. Unless the historical sources are factored in based on the written records from ancient times, the solution will not be accurate.

For example, many current theorists suggest that the massive edifice at Great Zimbabwe was built as recently as 800 years ago. There is abundant evidence to the contrary.

These buildings were constructed by the ancestors of the Shona tribes who still call this region their home. The earliest dates for settlement in the area by the Shona ancestors have been given as the fifth century, supposing it began initially as an agricultural economy. But there is no concrete proof that the date could not have been much earlier, and overlapped with the time frame of Solomon and the Queen of Sheba. The presence of the ancestors of the Shona in this region could have occurred much sooner.

The intervening centuries have left multiple layers of many civilizations. There is no reason to believe that in the eons of time, no one had ventured into this region prior to 500 A.D.

Most of the speculation about the time line of the Shona migration to this region has been the "armchair conjecture" of Europeans, who are themselves newcomers to this region of Africa. The Europeans, with few exceptions, only arrived here in the last two hundred years.

There are even current attempts to claim that Solomon and the Queen of Sheba are nothing more than fictional characters, despite written records that have come to us from many different cultures to prove otherwise.

Others suggest that if Great Zimbabwe is, in fact, the palace of the Queen of Sheba, and the nearby mines were the source of her country's exports to Solomon and other nations of that time, the buildings would not have survived at all. This is contradicted by the fact that the other palace of the Queen of Sheba near Aksum, in Ethiopia is still in a remarkably preserved enough state to identify the forty palace rooms, the perimeters, and the passageways. The courtyards and existing walls are enough to give us an idea of their former grandeur in ancient times.

There is ample evidence from history and the various records and texts that have come down to us, to suggest that Great Zimbabwe was an integral and central part of the ancient mines that operated in this area.

Carbon-14 Dating

The use of Carbon-14 dating has some specific limitations in the accurate dating of some materials. The Carbon-14 dating at Great Zimbabwe, for example, has shown an erratic data range for determining the origin of Great Zimbabwe. Some readings give it as originating as recently as the twelfth century A.D. Other readings have given it an originating date as early as the fourth century A.D. This shows a possible error range of 800 years, and is in no way able to be relied on as accurate.

Also, carbon 14 can only be used on material from biological sources of once-living things. This would apply to objects such as human or animal bones, or plant fibers used in the making of baskets.

To make an accurate measure, the archaeological layers from the most recent occupation of the site to the earliest habitation would have to be clearly delineated. There has been no accurate, controlled excavation of such layers of civilization at Great Zimbabwe.

Instead there has been a haphazard destruction of the top layers which are relevant only to the most recent inhabitants of the site in the past few centuries. Therefore, artifacts produced suggested dates moderately tied to the twelfth century.

The archaeological work to date in no way gives an accurate measurement of the time of origin of Great Zimbabwe. Historical data from ancient records and sources would place it much closer to 1000 B.C., or even earlier.

Further there are some other inherent problems with the accuracy of Carbon-14 dating. Carbon-14 in the atmosphere has fluctuated over time. Also, the earth's magnetic field affects the amount of Carbon-14 produced.

Beyond a certain point, most Carbon-14 is no longer detectable, because of degradation. Beyond a certain length of time, no accurate or relevant information can be detected. Scientists report errors with differentials as great as 3,000 years.

Protecting the Site

If only the inaccuracy of determining timelines was at stake, it would be forgivable. But the disregard of newcomers to the Great Zimbabwe site, especially in the last century, has amounted to little more than looting and plundering the sacred location. Random groups over time have engaged in voluntary digging, and carried off artifacts with abandon. The reckless digging damaged and obliterated clues necessary to determining the real time frames in which the buildings at Great Zimbabwe originated.

After Europeans descended upon the site in the past century, anyone who owned a shovel fancied himself an archaeologist. This same carelessness for national treasures was noted by Webber Ndoro in his article about Great Zimbabwe which appeared in *Scientific American*, in the December 1, 2004 issue. As he aptly observed,

> Europeans arrived, lured by visions of gold from Solomon's mines . . . It was then that the archaeological record became so damaged as to become largely undecipherable.

By 1891, callous and destructive digging had already caused significant damage at the site. In the process, the stratigraphy was damaged, and made it nearly impossible to determine the age by studying ground layers. Added to this was a thorough disregard for record keeping. Amateur archaeologists wreaked havoc with abandon. There was no restraint in the pillaging that destroyed the markers and clues that might have defined the true dates in the archeological records. This former damage was observed and reflected in the notes of James Theodore Bent, who attempted to map out his findings at the site.

The British South Africa Company, under the direction of Cecil Rhodes, had given W. G. Neal free rein to take gold at will from any archaeological site, and to discard, without appropriate records, any artifacts which did not suit his interests. Record keeping was non-existent. The reckless mistakes have destroyed vital clues that might have provided a real assessment of the origins of this remarkable architectural complex, and given us an accurate timeline.

Finally in 1928, the government passed laws to protect the site, but much significant damage had already been done.

Sometimes accidents and mishaps are unavoidable. This was pointed out by Webber Ndoro in his book *The Preservation of Great Zimbabwe*, published by ICCROM in 2005. He noted that an attempt to do carbon-14 dating entailed the removal of some small pieces of wood in the stone walls. This ultimately caused partial collapse in one of the walls. As Ndoro observed, "Such well-intentioned acts have led to most of the irreparable damage."

A vigilant approach needs to be maintained to preserve such world treasures. There is a need to respect the African people for whom these are not simply "tourist stops", but are their birthright, their sacred trust, and their cultural roots.

Exploring the Complex

Great Zimbabwe and its elaborate grounds comprise three separate architectural centers: The Hill Complex, the Great Enclosure, and the Valley Complex. These are believed by some to have existed in separate and sequential time periods, independently of each other.

The Great Zimbabwe, or "Stone House", is the largest of many smaller settlements throughout the area. The region is bound in the North by the Zambezi River and in the South by the Limpopo River. To the east is Mozambique.

The Great Zimbabwe complex, now a national park, stands at an elevation of 3,300 feet above sea level. On the horizon, the Chimanimani Mountains rise as a backdrop against the monument defined by time.

The Hill Complex

The Hill Complex is distinctive by the unusually huge mass of granite which surrounds the architecture like a protective fortress. It is also referred to as the "East Enclosure". This complex is believed to have been the oldest part of Great Zimbabwe. It is conservatively estimated to have been in use from the ninth to the thirteenth century AD. Some faulty archaeological work, destructive digging and irresponsible evaluations in this past century have brought the actual age of the structure into serious dispute.

Recently, serious researchers have found the origin designated in the ninth century to be highly inaccurate. They argue that the beginning lies closer to 1,500 BC at the latest. Of course there have been more recent habitations of Great Zimbabwe over time, especially in the late Iron Age, but they should not be mistaken as being the original occupants.

The Hill complex sits at an elevation of 262 feet above the surrounding terrain. The enclosure itself is 328 feet in length and 148 feet in width. The outer wall is 37 feet in height.

This high precipice on which the Hill Site is built is considered to have been a "royal" acropolis and the home to a long line of tribal chiefs. It is believed to have functioned as a temple, under the auspices of the ruler. It is considered the most sacred location on the Great Zimbabwe site.

Nearby, a dramatic boulder appears to have the striking shape and profile of the Zimbabwe bird, which is so revered in this nation.

The enclosure here originally had six pedestals, each of which was crowned with the "birds of Zimbabwe" – treasures promptly stripped from the site by Europeans in the past century. Some were pirated to museums, and one was taken by Cecil Rhodes, himself, to decorate his home. There is hope that all of these statues will be returned to the people of Zimbabwe to whom they rightfully belong. Some of the birds, as later discussed, have already been returned, but are not on display or exhibition at Great Zimbabwe at this time.

The significance and the ritual use of the birds is still undetermined.

The Great Enclosure

The Great Enclosure, also called the "Western Enclosure", is located south of the Hill Complex. This area is tentatively believed to have been inhabited from the thirteenth to the fifteenth centuries. The accuracy of its date of its origin, however, like that of the Hill Complex, are currently disputed. This is due to the damage caused by overzealous amateur archaeologists in the last century who compromised the site, and any serious attempts to accurately date it. These treasure hunters carried off gold and priceless artifacts as souvenirs. They disturbed the successive layers that contained the clues of the many rulers who occupied this site over time.

Most interesting here are the two elliptical walls which encircle the area. These massive granite walls are built without the benefit of mortar or any other binding materials. The walls are 820 feet in length, and have a height of 36 feet. Over a million blocks were used to create them. The sheer beauty of the ancient rock with its graceful curve is unique to this area of Zimbabwe.

The inner and outer walls create a unique passageway that is 180 feet in length. Between the inner and outer walls, there is an imposing rock tower shaped like a cone. It is thirty feet high and eighteen feet in diameter.

The circular enclosure, which is massive even by current standards, was called the "Imbahuru", which in the Kalanga language means, "House of the Great Woman." As mentioned earlier, this is believed to be alluding to the Queen of Sheba, who many believe lived here when she made this city the capital of her gold empire.

Long after the Queen of Sheba, the enclosure was believed to have housed the wives of the successive rulers.

There is evidence that some interior structures were once built inside the walls of the stone enclosure. These may have been some kind of mud and thatch dwellings which were seasonally replaced. There is no indication, however, that there has ever been a roof or ceiling of any kind.

The Valley Complex

There is a more random scattering of buildings in the ruins which lie in the Valley Complex. Although they are the most recent structures, they appear to be in greater disrepair. This area most likely housed the expanding population of citizens, while the other two complexes were designed for the leaders and people of higher rank.

The people who lived in the Valley Complex were still in close proximity to the ruler. These people may have staffed the working operations of Great Zimbabwe, and attended to the needs of the ruler. Also, it is possible that they worked in the nearby mines that are believed to have been the greatest source of income for Great Zimbabwe.

The prosperity brought by the gold trade supported many kingdoms over the centuries. The occupation in the valley complex appeared to end during the sixteenth century AD.

The Stone Birds of Zimbabwe

The significance of the eight stone Zimbabwe birds that graced the Eastern Enclosure of the Hill Complex is not immediately evident. This location marks the most sacred place at Great Zimbabwe, and suggests some religious purpose was intended.

The birds, carved in sleek soapstone, are each about sixteen inches in height, and originally were set atop columns forty inches in height.

The entire complex of stone buildings lies open to the sky – as if in a gesture of being receptive to that boundless and endless expanse of blue. Perhaps the birds are a tribute to Mwari, the Creator God of the Shona who lives in the sky, and is the "King of the Sky". He is the Protective Spirit who inhabits this place and protects it.

This connection with the sky is important to the Shona, because it represents a connection to Heaven and to the sacred ancestors who reside there. This is, above all, a sacred space.

The bird is called "Shiri ya Mwari" which means literally "The Bird of God". Is he perhaps the messenger who carries the prayers of the people to God himself?

The eight stone birds have wandered far from this peaceful home over the past years, but now all of them, except for one have come home to Zimbabwe.

Five of the birds went to the Cape Colony and were sold to Cecil Rhodes. These were returned to Zimbabwe in 1981 by the South African government. A sixth bird was bought by Cecil Rhodes and is still at his Cape Town home called *Groote Schuur*.

A seventh bird, taken by a missionary in 1907 and sold to a museum in Berlin, was returned ninety-six years later in 2003.

The eighth and final bird was always kept in Zimbabwe.

The bird appears to be the African fish eagle, also known as the Bateleur eagle. It was displayed on the South Rhodesian flag, and since independence was declared in 1980 it figures prominently on the national Zimbabwe flag. The bird bears a striking resemblance to the quetzal, a divine bird from pre-Columbian times which appears on the flag of Guatemala.

The focus on the sky, and the creatures who inhabit the sky, has alluded to possible extraterrestrial ties. Robert K. G. Temple in his book *The Sirius Mystery* published in 1977, speaks of the "Dogon" tribe in Mali which has an astronomical connection with the Sirius star system. Also, the race of amphibious beings called the Nommo, are said to have come from the stars. In West Africa they are called the "Zishwezi".

There is a common belief in "sky people" and "sky gods". These are part of folk tales by the Bushmen of the Kalahari, and tribes in Namibia and Zaire, who incorporate stories of the "men from the sky." The word "Zulu" means "people from the stars."

Figure G.

Early morning inside the Great Enclosure. Several centuries after the Queen of Sheba, tribal kings in the fourteenth and fifteenth centuries used this enclosure to house their many wives.

Chapter 7

THE BUILDERS OF GREAT ZIMBABWE

The Shona, a group of the Bantu people, today occupy Zimbabwe and neighboring South African countries.

There are five main language groups: the Karanga, Ndau, Manyika, Zesuru and the Korekore.

The two primary regional divisions include the Eastern Shonas, and the Bakalanga, also known as the Western Shonas. There is mutual language compatibility among the main dialects in the east and west.

There are almost 11 million Shona today including the Southern or Karanga Shona, the Rozvi, the Zezuru and the Northern Shona called the Korekore.

Several sub-divisions comprise these primary groups.

The use of the word "Shona" did not come into common use until the 1800's. However, the Shona people had identified for many centuries with the Monomotapa kingdom – the most significant of the African kingdoms.

The Shona people were often referred to during that time as Karanga or Kalanga, which now comprise separate sub-groups.

What is most important is that these different groups under the current designation "Shona" have a rich common culture and keen memory of ancient times which have survived in their customs, and their verbal and written histories.

The Shonas were the skilled builders of Great Zimbabwe, the largest structure built in stone south of the Sahara.

For a long time English colonialists and explorers at the astounding Great Zimbabwe attempted to claim foreigners had built the magnificent stone edifices. This attempt to deny the skilled genius of the native people eventually failed.

There was simply no evidence that anyone other than the Shona people had created the elegant rock creations that today rise up above the green hills thirty miles from the modern town of Masvingo.

Even in pre-colonial times, the export of both gold and copper were well established in this region. The gold production of the Zimbabwe mines is believed by many significant researchers to date back thousands of years.

The suggestions of Great Zimbabwe having been involved with mining, has supported the belief that the great riches that the Queen of Sheba presented to King Soloman – in particular the large quantity of gold – came from the mines in this region. There is also speculation that it was here at Great Zimbabwe that the Queen of Sheba lived and made the city her capital.

She is also purported to have had properties and holdings in Egypt, Ethiopia, and what is now Yeman in the Saudi Arabian peninsula. However, none of these places had extensive mining deposits, nor could have provided the amount of gold that was extensively mined in this region adjacent to Great Zimbabwe.

The mines of Great Zimbabwe in this region have been in existence since well before the time of Israel's King David. He, himself, imported a significant amount of gold from this area, as Biblical accounts attest.

This is a strong indication that this was the same source of King Solomon's gold, and that Great Zimbabwe was the processing and export site of King Solomon's Mines.

The Great Enclosure at Great Zimbabwe, was known in the Kalanga language as the "House of the Great Woman". Only the Queen of Sheba, at that time, had such a great power or reputation. She is certainly the woman spoken of at Great Zimbabwe. She had ruled her nation from the age of fifteen, and had secured, protected and expanded the wealth of her people by her continued efforts.

Before the Portuguese arrived, the Mutapa State had already established significant foreign gold trade with East Asia and Arabia.

This had been brought about by the Rozwi, one of the clans of the early Shona who established Monomotapa – the thriving empire which was created by Mwene Motapa, a native chief who brought together the many different tribes and factions to reinforce a solidarity among the people in Zimbabwe. This remarkable unified kingdom stretched from the Kalihari desert in the west to the Indian Ocean.

Today, it is estimated that 70 percent of Shona are Christians. However, their traditional beliefs are still a part of their rich and ancient culture.

There is still a great respect for the "Vadzimu" who are the ancestor spirits, who embody what is sacred to the Shona. Integral to the family are the "mudzimu" who are the ancestral family spirits who watch over their respective families. In some sacred ceremonies, a medium called an "n'anga" can communicate with the spirits who live in what is believed to be a world parallel to our own.

The representations of totems are also a significant part of ancient customs for the Shona. These are still acknowledged and respected today.

One of the totems, for example, is the Fish Eagle – identified as the bird immortalized in statues at Great Zimbabwe. This is the bird which is represented on the national flag of Zimbabwe. Other totems include the Zebra, the Lion, and the Crocodile among others. Therefore, those people with the same totem have descended from one common ancestor.

This common heritage governs to a great extent who may marry, since a Shona is not allowed to marry a person with the same totem. It also involves precedents and rules with respect to who may preside at burial ceremonials.

Some anthropologists have dated human occupation of Africa to 7 million years ago. On the other hand, substantial numbers of people believe that human existence did not extend back more than 6,000 to 10,000 years. It is no wonder then, that there is a controversy over the dating of Great Zimbabwe. But it is clear that dating it consistently to the eleventh century A.D. makes no sense, when references to the great gold produced at that center in Africa were made long before King David of the Israelites. This is confirmed by sources from Egypt, Arabia and Ethiopia to name a few.

The origins and dating of the Bantu language, itself, began in central West Africa, moving to the East. Finally it moved southward to the Zimbabwe area. But amazingly the language, itself, was in use as early as 1000 BC. This aligns with the time frame of King Solomon and the Queen of Sheba.

Figure H.

**This section of the Hill Complex was believed to be
holy ground and used for rituals and prayers.**

Chapter 8

ARK OF THE COVENANT

There is some speculation that the Ark of the Covenant is at Great Zimbabwe, concealed in some way. Although that is not the position or belief of this author, this chapter will deal with some speculations and claims that have been made about the alleged location, and examine their authenticity.

Let us begin at the beginning of the Ark of the Covenant story. According to the Bible, about 3,500 years ago on Mount Sinai God instructed Moses in how to build the Ark. This sacred vessel was to hold the tablets of the Ten Commandments, his brother Aaron's rod, and a jar of manna to commemorate the crossing of the Israelites in the desert during the Exodus.

For 400 years from the time of the Exodus to the time of King Solomon, the ark of the covenant was in the hands of the Israelites. During the sojourn in the desert, it was placed in the center of encampments, where the twelve tribes were arranged around the tabernacle in an established order.

At the time of the Exodus, only the priests of the tribe of Levi were allowed to touch the tabernacle. There was always a protecting barrier to keep others at a distance. The directives not to touch the ark indicated that it presented possible danger if dealt with recklessly. This is indicated also in the specific directives of how to interact with the ark. There were elaborate rules for its use, for example, the proper procedure for transporting the ark by means of the special poles attached to the sides of the ark.

The explicit building instructions are given in Exodus 25, 10-11:

> And you shall make an ark of acacia wood; two and a half cubits shall be its length, a cubit and a half its width, and a cubit and a half its height. And you shall overlay it with pure gold, inside and out you shall overlay it, and shall make on it a molding of gold all around.

God gave further instructions regarding the rings of gold that were to be placed in the four corners on each side of the ark, and the golden-covered poles of acacia wood which were to be inserted into those rings for carrying. He also directed that the poles should remain always in the ark, and never be removed.

In *Exodus* 26:19, the instructions resemble an engineering diagram:

> Forty sockets of silver under the twenty boards. Two sockets under each of the boards for its two tenons to be coupled at the bottom and the top.

The text continues with an array of other requirements including hooks, bars, knobs, utensils, and sockets of bronze. God told Moses to have the workmen "wash their hands and feet, lest they die." He also directed them to "add oil, and add water."

He told them, in *Exodus* 25:22, that upon completion of this work,

> There I will meet with you, and I will speak with you from above the mercy seat, from between the two cherubim . . . about everything which I will give you in commandments to the children of Israel.

The specific nature of the instructions, and the materials used, have led some scientists to speculate that the ark of the covenant, when assembled, was some kind of radio, transmitter, or large battery, capable of high energy levels or charges. They say that this was the reason for the precautions given for washing hands and feet and using certain chemicals, to somehow avoid contamination.

Some have suggested that since gold is a conductor, it is possible that the delivery of electrical charges, when grounded, could create bursts of electrical radiation. The components, and the respective parts could also have acted as a capacitor.

This issue was addressed by Roger Isaacs in the article "*Incense Protected Biblical Israelites from Radiation Burn*" (Huffington Post, July 30, 2015). He suggested that the use of incense and other specific chemical compounds was to deactivate radiation which could be released when handling the Ark. This would explain Biblical references to people who died or became severely ill upon contact with the machine. This would also account for the use of special uniforms or specified garments to be worn when in contact with the Ark, and the strict regulations surrounding its use.

The Biblical texts make repeated mention of God's explicit demands to avoid touching the ark. This was of course the purpose of its being transported by the carrying poles. The general perception, observing its effects on those who violated God's order, was that it could result in electrocution, burns, sickness and death. All of these suggest the presence of severe radiation effects.

The ark of the covenant was carried into a number of battles. The most well known was the renowned battle of Jericho, in which the ark of the covenant, accompanied by the trumpets of the soldiers, was carried around Jericho until the walls of the city crumbled and the city was destroyed.

The account in *Samuel*, chapter 4-6, suggests again the tremendous power of the ark of the covenant to destroy when mishandled. This occurred when the Israelites battled with the Philistines. The Israelites lost 30,000 men, and the ark of the covenant was captured by the Philistines, who brought it to the city of Ashdod. 1 *Samuel* 5:6 tells us:

> The Lord's hand was heavy on the people of Ashdod; He brought devastation on them and afflicted them with tumors. When the people saw what was happening, they said, the ark of the god of Israel must not stay with us.

Then they sent the ark to the city of Gath, where everyone there developed tumors. Then the people in Gath rebelled, and the Ark was sent to the city of Ekron.

> As the ark of God was entering Ekron, the people cried out, 'They have brought the ark of the god of Israel around to kill us and our people'. So they called together the rulers of the Philistines and said, "Send the ark away; let it go back to its own place, or it will kill us and our people." For death had filled the city with panic. Those who did not die were affected with tumors.

Samuel 4-6

After seven months, the ark had been sent from town to town, and the injuries and deaths continued in each town. Finally, the Philistine rulers put the ark of the covenant on a cart pulled by two oxen and sent it, without a driver, toward the Israelite town of Beth Shemesh. They watched from afar until the cart reached that town. By this time, they were breathing a sigh of relief.

The Israelites who saw the cart approaching with the ark of the covenant were thrilled to have their treasure returned to them. However, some of them looked inside the ark, and seventy of them were struck dead.

These accounts establish, certainly, the great power able to be generated by the ark of the covenant.

The current location of the art of the covenant is a continuing puzzle. There are any number of suggested scenarios. What we do know is that around the time of the Babylonian attack under King Nebuchadnezzar in 587 BC, the ark was still apparently in Solomon's Temple.

The most enduring story is that expressed earlier in this book about Solomon's son Melelik having carried the Ark to Aksum where it became the basis for the conversion of Ethiopia, and initiated the Solomonic dynasty of Ethiopia's kings. That unbroken succession of the Solomonic kings lasted for over 3,000 years, until it was terminated in this century with the death of Haile Selassie.

Some accounts said that when Menelik took the ark from Jerusalem prior to the Babylonian invasion of 587 BC, a "recreated model imitation" was left in its place. Therefore, the original would still be at Aksum today in Ethiopia, where it is in the Chapel of the Tablet, in the Church of St. Mary of Zion. There have been a series of successive guardians. Each of these guardians serves for life. One observation has been that the priests who have been chosen to guard the ark have, according to some accounts, tended to have suffered radiation-type poisoning, burns, blindness and short lifespans. Whether this is legend or fact, it is a story that persists.

Other stories abound. One is that the Babylonians took the Ark from the temple and carried it away with them. However, there did not appear to be any historical claim by the Babylonians that this had occurred. The other story is that the Babylonians destroyed the ark when they burned down the temple and the city.

The book of 2 *Maccabees*, says that Jeremiah had been warned in a dream that the Babylonians were intending to invade Jerusalem. It suggested that he took the ark of the covenant to Mount Nebo, and concealed it in a cave.

Tudor Parfitt, in his book *The Lost Ark of the Covenant* (Harper Collins; 2008) tried to establish with genetic research that the Lemba tribe of Africa were part of the lost tribe of Israel. His supposition was that they had brought the ark of the covenant to Africa, possibly to Great Zimbabwe. Lemba traditions state that it "self-destructed" about 700 years ago, and that they rebuilt it with what was left, and put it in a cave in the Dunghe mountains. Ultimately it ended up in a Harare museum in 2007.

Partly Parfitt based his assumption on the Lemba people's story of the drum called the "ngoma lungundu", which literally translates to "voice of God," and was said to have made a sound like thunder. The difficulty lies in the fact that the wooden item, despite having possible carrying rings, has no resemblance to the ark as described in *Exodus*.

Another proposed location for the ark is that it is in the beautiful and impressive Chartres Cathedral built in France during the twelfth century A.D. This idea was promoted by Louis Charpentier in his book *Mysteries of Chartres Cathedral*, when he suggested that the Templar Knights acquired the ark of the covenant during the Crusades, and that it is now concealed somewhere in the massive Chartres Cathedral.

Another theory was put forward by Grant Jeffrey in his book *The New Temple and the Second Coming* (Waterbrook Press, 2007). He stated that the original ark of the covenant was in Aksum, Ethiopia, as tradition supports, but that it was transported to Israel in 1991. He said that a group of some orthodox rabbis in Jerusalem called the Temple Institute have control of the ark of the covenant, and that it is protected under the Temple Mount in a hidden vault or chamber. One argument against this would be that a transfer of the ark from the centuries-old site of Aksum to Israel would seem to have been unlikely. If the ark has been under guard in Aksum, Ethiopia for 3,000 years, it would not likely have been removed without protest or notice in 1991.

The only story that appears to have consistency over time would be the holding of the ark of the covenant at Aksum.

Figure I.

Sunset view inside the Great Enclosure at Great Zimbabwe.

Printed in the United States
By Bookmasters